How To Retire Early Through Dividend Investing

By
Marc Guberti

Your Free Gift

As a way of thanking you for your purchase, I am offering you a free **Income Spreadsheet** you can use to keep track of your income and expenses.

As you will learn throughout the book, keeping track of your income and expenses is essential to building up your dividend portfolio.

If you are interested in tracking your money, then I recommend getting your free **Income Spreadsheet** which comes with insights that will help you make smarter money decisions.

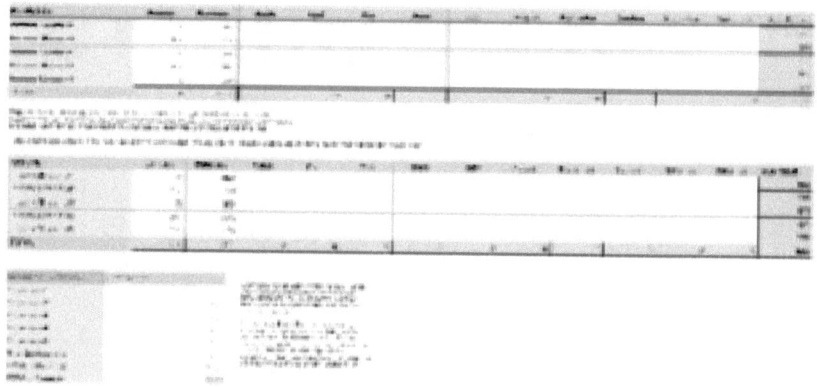

marcguberti.com/income-spreadsheet

Table Of Contents

Introduction

What do we do with our money after we've received it? Statistically speaking, most people spend that money. In fact, 60% of Americans spend the same amount of money or more money than they make.

Financial literacy isn't taught in most schools. This explains why many people make poor decisions with their money that hurt their chances of an early retirement.

This is why we will start this book by focusing on financial discipline. If you can't look at your money without thinking of how you'll spend it, you won't retire early from dividend investing.

Dividend investing isn't the only investment vehicle that allows you to retire early. However, it's the one we will cover in this book. Many people have misconceptions about how dividend investing works and how it builds up wealth over-time. Others don't know what to look for in a dividend stock.

By the end of this journey, you'll know the tools and resources you can use to build up your financial discipline and invest your way to an early retirement.

Part 1

Saving More Than You Spend

The simplest way to approach investing your way to retirement is by looking t the math. The key to an early retirement is to have your dividends cover all of your living expenses. If your dividends can pay for food, your home, taxes, and everything else, you can retire right now.

The dividends can build up to include vacations, experiences, and other things like that, but retirement in its basic sense is passive income that exceeds your living expenses.

The three ways to speed up your retirement are by earning more money, investing more of that earned money (a.k.a. not spending it…and not just saving all of it either), and investing that money at higher returns.

Earning more money helps, but that extra money doesn't do you any good if you don't invest it. Since most people don't think about the simple math from earlier, they think they need to win the lottery and receive $1 million to retire from dividend investing…or something of that nature.

You'd think that if you won the lottery, you'd be set. That couldn't be further from the truth.

Sure, winning $1 million from the lottery would be incredible and you could buy yourself a house and a few other toys with that money. Most people do just that…and that's where the problem is.

The Penny Hoarder wrote an article detailing 21 lottery winners who ended off worse because they won the lottery. Many of these lottery winners won $1 million. But some of the winners featured in the article won over $100 million and still end up broke in a few years. Houses, vacations, jewelry, drugs, and casinos were some of the places that money went to.

These stories aren't outliers either. Most people quickly burn through the lottery money.

Winning the lottery isn't a bad thing, but it can be devastating over the long-term if the wrong person wins.

Here's one thing to remember about money…it doesn't make you a better or worse person. Rather, money amplifies who you already are. If you are a kind, discipline person, and you suddenly make a ton of money, you suddenly become kinder and more disciplined. If on the other hand, a nasty person makes money, that person becomes nastier.

With that in mind, more money won't change your spending habits. Waiting to get a big raise or extra stream of income to change your habits is a poor strategy that relies on an external change rather than an internal change. Internal changes are where the magic happens. External changes eventually give way to who we are on the inside and what our hardwired habits tell us to do.

Everyone has a different financial situation. The goal of this book is to give people some action steps regardless of their situation. Some people can invest $100s each month. Other people can't afford to do that. If you find yourself financially struggling, all I ask is that you find at least a penny to spend on a fractional share of a dividend stock or a fund that provides a dividend. Robinhood makes this very easy to do with any stock and some brokers will let you buy a penny's worth of one of their fund's shares.

You can even get a free stock if you join Robinhood through this link: join.robinhood.com/marcg665.

I also get a free stock when you join through the above link, so it is a win-win if you feel like you're on a tight budget.

I got a free share of Glu Mobile when I joined Rohinhood. It's not a high-end company but it's a free $5.90. You can either hold onto the company Robinhood gives you or sell it and use the proceeds to buy a dividend stock.

For people who are financially struggling, the penny is more symbolic than anything else and will officially put you in the game of dividend investing. That penny won't help you retire, but it will inspire you. A free stock from Robinhood also helps with building up your portfolio.

Regardless of your financial status, it's important to think of what happens to the money we make. Some of our money will go towards living expenses. But where is the rest of that money going?

For a long time, I played video games. While some of the video games I played were very enjoyable, many of the video games I got were barely used. I played some for about a year and then stopped playing them. If I had to pay for all of those video games and had the financial discipline I had now, I'd not buy at least 90% of those video games.

Some people want the luxury car, the fashion statement, and the accessories. I would never spend $10,000 on a Rolex Watch, but some people do just that.

I'm currently 22 years old and without a driver's license. Anyone who knows me knows that it's not because I am lazy. Part of the reason is that I spend most of my time working on my business or with my family and local friends. Another part of the reason is that I'm in no rush to pay car expenses. I'm not buying a car for myself until I first buy my own property.

I understand that the majority of people need a car, but I wanted to share my perspective. Some people who read this book will be young enough to make those kinds of decisions and are in that "If I could start all over" position scenario people think of as they get older and wiser.

Give Yourself Less Money To Play With

It baffles me that some people keep on spending money and it feels like spending is a part of their identity. They can't imagine a life where they don't have the money to spend on things they'll buy now and not care about later.

It is important to reduce your spending money to retire sooner and think more about your spending habits. This spending money is different from the money that is meant to be saved and invested.

The easiest way to reduce your spending money is through automatic investments. You can arrange with your bank and broker to automatically invest a certain amount of money each month. If this money leaves your bank account before you get the chance to spend it, you have less spending money and more money invested into different assets.

Automatic investing is an easy set-up that reaps many benefits. The automatic investments should either go to a fund with a proven dividend record or one that mimics a major index like the S&P 500 which is my favorite.

The automatic investments make you wiser about the money you have to spend. Do you really need to go to high-end restaurants or can you make good food yourself? Do you really need Disney+, Netflix, and the other one, or can you trim it down a bit? Are you going to the gym enough to continue paying the membership fee?

These are some of the many questions you should ask about the money you currently spend. I guarantee that anyone who keeps asking questions like the ones above will come across a few ways that they currently spend their money in areas where they shouldn't be.

Giving yourself less spending money than usual makes you think more about each purchase and some of the recurring payments you've committed yourself to.

Giving yourself less money to play with will also makes you think of why you spend the way you do. Do you need to watch the movie when it hits theaters or can you wait for it to be on Disney+?

We have a variety of reasons for our purchasing decisions, but if they align with any of the upcoming reasons, you should stay away from the investment:

Bad reason #1: The desire to impress others

For most of us, it's not that often when we see a Lamborghini on the road. When we do, we notice. The Lamborghini does the same exact things as the Toyota…it drives you from Point A to Point B, shields you from the rain, and other basic stuff.

The only difference is that having a Lamborghini is impressive and people will compliment you for your car and want to know more about you. That's nice and all. But do you really have to spend around half a million dollars to create that effect? And let's not forget about the higher costs for keeping your Lamborghini versus keeping the Toyota. A Lamborghini's annual payments look very different from that of a Toyota.

A Rolex watch and a smartphone both tell time. One of them can be bought for over $10,000, and no…that's not how much the new iPhone costs. A smartphone does much more than just tell time, but if you take it out from your pocket, you get the time. You can also buy a much cheaper watch if you're into watches.

I get it. Not everyone has the kind of money to throw at a Lamborghini or a Rolex. However, if you buy anything…

whether it be a shirt, pair of sneakers, accessory, or anything else for the sole reason of impressing others, don't buy it.

Buying things to impress others is a fleeting feeling. Even if you impress for a brief moment, you'll feel compelled to impress again…and that means spending more money on an unnecessary item you'll forget about later. You can find yourself spending money on things to impress society rather than things that you truly want and make more sense. This is how spending money becomes a dangerous part of some people's identity.

Bad reason #2: Boosting your confidence

I am all for being confident and looking for ways to boost your confidence. With that said, your wallet is the wrong place to look for extra confidence. The only purchase that makes sense for this category are books and other educational resources that can help you here. However, there is still a limit to how many books and other resources you can get before you have to do something about your life and circumstances to boost your confidence.

This is similar to the Lamborghini and Rolex examples from before. Having one of those things can boost confidence in the short-term because people may take you more seriously.

However, those things ware off the longer you own them. It was really exciting when you got your new smartphone or computer. You felt more confident and advanced. Now it just blends in the background. You still use it, but not with the same excitement as Day 1. That's what eventually happens to all of the "stuff" we get.

You can feel sharper in the short term if you get an Apple product, but that external feeling goes away after you've used the product enough times. Products cater to our external feelings which only offer short-term solutions to problems where we need long-term solutions. You only get the long-term solutions by looking internally at yourself and making the changes that need to be made.

You can see this in effect when people buy things as a form of therapy. It feels good to have the ability to buy things, and some people go too far with this power to feel better about themselves when they hit a rough patch.

You can also see confidence boosting and impressing others by buying into the cool and latest trends that all of your other friends have bought into. Don't buy something just because a lot of people you know have bought it too.

Bad reason #3: You are addicted

Spending is a way of life which brings purpose to your life. If you relate to that, you're addicted to spending and accumulating stuff rather than accumulating wealth. If you view your salary or income stream as spending money, automatic investing will be a great starting point.

If you are addicted to spending, start surrounding yourself with people who will keep you accountable so you avoid the spending crave.

Justifying One Of My Purchases

With all of this said, many purchases beyond living expenses still make sense. The three best purchasing decisions are the following:

1. The purchase fits in the living expenses category
2. The purchase helps you accomplish a goal you've committed yourself to over a long period of time that improves your life in some way
3. The purchase provides you with a great experience

Let me give you an example of a purchase that can seem high end but can still be justified.

I have been running for about 8 years now and I can easily see myself continuing to run for the rest of my life. Running is high quality fitness and I have fun doing it.

Now I run a bunch of marathons and half-marathons each year. My goal is to run in all six of the Marathon Majors before I turn 30. That means I need to run a fast marathon time.

I will have to break 3 hours in a marathon just to have the ability to submit an application for the Boston Marathon. The more my time is under 3 hours, the more likely I am to get accepted and be able to run at that marathon. At this current stage, it's just a matter of me not walking after Mile 22. If I can do that, I'd have no problem hitting the time I need to hit.

For the Berlin Marathon, I'd have to run a marathon in under 2 hours and 45 minutes. So I did what any marathoner thinks about doing or has already done.

I got myself a pair of VaporFlys. These sneakers don't come cheap. They're $250 a pair which is more than most sneakers. From a comparison standpoint, I bought 3 pair of training sneakers for a grand total of $90. They were on a discount, the sneakers feel good, and that still comes at less than the cost of a single pair of the Nike Pegasus, so I got them at that price.

The $250 seems excessive until you realize it aligns with Decision #2 I'd use to justify a purchase. I have been running for 8 years, and every runner wants a better time. In my case, I need a specific time to achieve my goals and qualify for certain events. That's where the VaporFlys come in. I still train as hard as I have, but the VaporFly advantage is real.

Watch any competitive marathon and you will witness a sea of green and pink sneakers. The more competitive the marathon is, the more endless this green and pink sea will seem. Also, it's the sneaker of choice for the runners who win the big marathon events…including Eliud Kipchoge when he ran the first sub 2 hour marathon.

The sneaker doesn't suddenly turn a bad runner into a great runner. Rather, it gives a runner who wears them that extra boost that can be the difference between qualifying and not qualifying for an event.

This is different from just buying a pair of VaporFlys, not being a runner, and just walking around in them because they look cool and people think you're fast because you're the guy or gal with the VaporFlys.

I don't want people to think I am fast. I just want to be fast.

When I thought of the purchase, I thought of how that $250 could go into dividend stocks that give me an extra $7.50 each year that will compound over time (assuming a 3% yield). Regardless of the purchase size, this is how I think, and it's how you need to think as a dividend investor.

That's why I spend almost zero money on personal stuff. The VaporFlys were a special exception because they help with a meaningful goal in my life.

Buying digital currency in a video game that you're likely to stop playing in about a year doesn't quite fit the bill...unless you are into esports, that's how you make your living, and you think buying the digital currency will help with creating better YouTube, Twitch, and/or Mixer content.

I bring up this justifiable purchase because while you build up your dividend investing portfolio, you don't want to completely deprive yourself even when the purchase makes sense. After living expenses, at least 90% of my money goes into my portfolio or back into my business. The restriction I put on my spending money forces me to make better decisions with it such as when I purchased a pair of VaporFlys.

Even when you qualify for the Boston Marathon, you still have to pay a fee to run in that race. I know that fee can turn into more dividend stocks but I am still paying that fee because running the Boston Marathon is a meaningful life goal for me.

Tapping Into Your Long-Term Thinking

It's difficult for people to decide how much to save, invest, and spend. On one hand, you want to invest because investing will help future you's finances. On the other hand, investing gives present you less money to spend.

The reason people opt to spend money is because we live in the present and not everyone thinks in the long-term. In the long-term, you've got bills to pay, children and grandchildren you will hopefully want to spend time with, and an entire world to travel if you're into that type of lifestyle. In the short-term, the latest trends and products compete to get your hard earned dollar.

The key to financial discipline is to tap into your long-term thinking. Here are some simulations to get you thinking in the long-term.

#1: Your house is on fire. What are the first things you're grabbing? Is there anything you'd rush back into the house for if you forgot it? What are you leaving behind and why? The things you leave behind in this example already ate at your investment money, and some of them eat at your investment money each month. Some things like plates are replaceable which is why leaving those behind makes sense, but I'm in no rush to replace video game controllers. Some of the items you'd let burn in this example can be sold on eBay for extra money you can use to invest in your future.

#2: Don't like your job? In this case, you could listen to my Ditch The Job Podcast to discover how you can ditch your job and make more money starting your own business. But in this example, let's say you're stuck at your job and your living expenses are $4,000/mo. You have to continue this job for 40 years and then you can retire because the living expenses aren't going away anytime soon. If you stash away $100 each month and invest in dividend stocks, you may be able to retire 10 years early and make more dividend income than the salary at your jobs. Is craving to your short-term pleasures worth an extra 10 years at the job you hate?

#3: A big expense is coming up…whether it be college tuition, your first house, or a car, something big is coming. A dividend portfolio can help you pay these expenses with dividend income and stock appreciation. Spending money instead of investing it will naturally hold you back from making big purchases and advancements in life. A lack of financial education combined with student debt is a big reason why many people find themselves delaying big moves such as buying a house or marrying. It's also one of the reasons why so many more people rent versus buying their own property. These big expenses are bound to come up whether they're 1 year away or 20 years away. Start planning for them now instead of realizing you can't afford them later on. If you can't afford them later on, you'll be holding yourself and your entire family back from moving forward

I hope these examples help you think more over the long-term. To truly quantify what long-term thinking looks like, I'm going to share with you what happens to $1,000 you invest today at an annual 8% return. This is a commonly used example which is why it's the last example I'm using for this part of the book, but the growth is still incredible.

Year 1: $1,080
Year 5: $1,469.33
Year 10: $2,158.92
Year 20: $4,660.96
Year 30: $10,062.66

All of these figures assume you invest the $1,000 and do not invest another dollar. The more dollars you invest, the higher your return becomes. When factoring in monthly investments, the returns get dramatically higher.

Put Your Money Into Perspective

Before I make any purchase, I think about what that money could do for me in my portfolio. If I want to buy a shirt for $20, I immediately think of the different stocks I could buy for $20.

That $20 gets me 6 shares of Libsyn with some money left over (it's one of the few stocks I like that doesn't offer a dividend).

From a dividend investing standpoint, $20 gets me almost half of a share of Cisco. When I bought the VaporFlys for

$250, I saw that $250 and thought of the 5 TD Ameritrade shares I could have added to my portfolio.

While I justified buying the VaporFlys, I only use them for races and 1-2 workouts each month to still feel comfortable in them and preserve them in the process. That way, I don't have to buy them as frequently which means fewer $250 purchases. On other days I run in sneakers that won't cost as much to replace.

I'd rather have 3 shares of Cisco than 7 shirts that I barely wear. If you think this way with all of your spending decisions, you'll make fewer mistakes and get more conscious about each purchasing decision you make.

The reason most people overspend is because they don't know their numbers. A few years ago, I overspent on some assistants when more affordable options were available. I didn't think of it at the time until I saw how much I spent and how much I could have saved with a different approach. I could have saved at least $1,000 with a different approach. If I thought of that $1,000 as 50 shares of Bank of America (at the time, $1,000 would have been able to buy 50 shares of BAC), I would have spent my money very differently.

The assistants were an investment into my business, so I don't entirely consider it a waste of money. However, I could have been more productive with how I was spending my money and which assistants I chose to hire.

Mistakes like these happen. You can let them drag you down or you can simply learn from them. Learning from your mistakes and evading the same ones twice will build up your financial discipline and set you up for wealth later down the road.

Part 2

The Dividend Investing Strategy Revealed

We started by sharing how you can boost your financial discipline. At the end of the day, everyone needs enhanced financial discipline because temptations come up again and again. Towards the end, I mentioned a few dividend stocks I like at the time of writing this book.

The great thing about reliable dividend stocks is that even if the stock depreciates, you continue getting the dividend and can wait for the stock to climb back up. If the stock depreciates significantly without drastic changes to the fundamental business model, you can buy more shares at a discount.

Granted, there is a chance that a business cuts a dividend or goes out of business entirely. In the span of one year, GE cut its dividend by 96% from an annualized dividend of $0.96

per share to $0.04 per share. Granted GE's business and its financials were hit hard and the danger signs were there.

GE's net income was starting to take a deep dive into the negative the year of their first dividend cut from an annualized $0.96 per share to an annualized $0.48 per share. This cut happened at the end of the year and was followed by the drastic and sudden drop to an annualized dividend of $0.04 per share.

In January 2017, GE announced it would cut 12,000 jobs which isn't a good sign for future expansion. The dividend was cut in half at the end of that year.

That's not to say every company that cuts jobs will end up cutting its dividend, but if the company is in financial trouble, it will be harder for the company to continue tapping into some of their earnings to pay investors.

When a company has piling expenses and its revenue can't keep up, that company naturally looks for ways to cut down on expenses. Hence the job cuts.

Reducing the dividend also reduces expenses, but then a company also loses investors. A cut dividend reduces people's faith in the company which usually leads to a selloff.

While we enjoy receiving dividends, we must not forget that these dividends come at the expense of the company. If the company can't pay the dividends anymore, we don't get dividends from that company's stock anymore.

That is the risk of the game. As long as you stay educated about each company you invest in, you are less likely to fall into a GE investor's scenario. You can also invest in a fund that pays a dividend and stay educated on the fund rather than all of the companies.

With the risks now addressed, it's time to talk about the dividend investing strategy and how it pays well in the long-term.

The Different Ways You Make More Money From Dividend Investing

When you invest in a dividend stock, you receive a monthly, quarterly, semi-annual, or annual dividend. Most companies pay out dividends quarterly while some companies and funds give out dividends at different frequencies.

Let's say you buy a share of Cisco which currently pays an annualized $1.40 per share. You buy a share of Cisco and receive the $1.40 in four quarterly payments of $0.35 each quarter.

Most people know about this part of making money with dividend stocks…you get the dividend. However, most people don't know how the hidden ways dividend investors get paid.

Most people look at an annualized dividend of $1.40 per share and think they'll end up with $14 at the end of 10 years from one share of Cisco. However, you'll end up with more than you think over the 10 year period.

The first hidden way dividend investors get paid is through dividend reinvestment programs (DRIPs). Instead of taking the cash, the dividend investor will take the dividend and reinvest it into the stock.

To make the math easier, let's say Cisco trades at $45 per share and stays at that exact price point for 10 years. I wrote this book towards the end of 2019 so $45 is a reasonable price point for that timeframe.

The annualized $1.40 dividend is paid out in quarterly dividend payments of $0.35 per share. That $0.35 gets you an extra 0.0077 shares of Cisco to up your total to 1.0077 shares. When Cisco pays out its next dividend of $0.35 per share, you don't get $0.35. Instead, you get paid $0.3527 because of that fractional share you have. Now you have 1.0155 shares of Cisco after you reinvest your second dividend payment.

If you repeat the reinvesting and everything else stays the same over 10 years, you end up with 1.363 shares of Cisco. The fractional 0.3633 share can be sold for $16.34 for a 16.77% gain just by reinvesting in fractional Cisco shares assuming everything else stays the same.

However, these is one more factor that determines how much money dividend investors make, and it's the most important factor. That most important factor is the dividend growth rate.

It's common practice for companies to raise their dividend each year to signal to investors that they are still doing well. If a company doesn't raise their dividend or drastically reduces their dividend growth rate, it is often a red flag and can indicate that the company is in trouble or slowing down.

Cisco currently raises its dividend every April. I looked back at the dividend growth over the past five years and discovered that the average growth rate for those 5 years was 13.15%. Cisco is a cyclical stock and it raised its dividend at a lower rate in 2019 so we will assume a growth rate of 10% for this example.

Not only does an assumed 10% growth rate make the calculations easier, but you will also find that companies will grow their dividend at a lower rate as they become more mature. Companies that start off by increasing their dividend by 20% each year eventually find themselves in 10% territory or a little below that standard.

You can't keep on raising the dividend at a high rate forever if you don't keep growing at a rate that can sustain the dividend.

In our example, let's assume the Cisco dividend will grow at a rate of 10% each year for the entire 10 years. Here's what the quarterly payments look like each year:

2019: $0.35 per share

2020: $0.385 per share

2021: $0.425 per share

2022: $0.465 per share

2023: $0.51 per share

2024: $0.565 per share

2025: $0.62 per share

2026: $0.68 per share

2027: $0.75 per share

2028: $0.825 per share

If you do all of the calculations yourself, you'll realize that not all of those returns are perfect 10% returns. This is to reflect that most companies round to the nearest cent or half cent for their dividend payments. So far Cisco has only rounded to the nearest cent rather than the nearest half cent, but I included the half cent to demonstrate that it is a scenario and make the math a little more accurate.

Now let's go into how many shares you would have at the end of each year assuming you received all of the dividend payments from 2019.

Again, we are assuming Cisco stays at $45/share for the entire 10 years. Appreciation and depreciation will impact how many shares you receive when you reinvest your dividends. If a stock appreciates, your dividends get you fewer shares. If a stock depreciates, your dividends get you more shares.

The ticker symbol of Cisco is CSCO which is why I will be using CSCO for this example.

2019: 1.031 shares of CSCO
2020: 1.067 shares of CSCO
2021: 1.108 shares of CSCO
2022: 1.155 shares of CSCO
2023: 1.208 shares of CSCO
2024: 1.270 shares of CSCO
2025: 1.341 shares of CSCO
2026: 1.424 shares of CSCO
2027: 1.521 shares of CSCO
2028: 1.636 shares of CSCO

1.636 shares of Cisco is more than the 1.363 shares we had when we just factored dividend reinvestments. Going from 1.363 shares to 1.636 shares is a built-in 20% increase from the dividend growth rate. The fractional 0.636 share can be exchanged for $28.62 which is more than double the initial $14 we thought we were getting.

Furthermore, the share you got in 2019 had an annualized dividend of $1.40. Assuming a 10% growth rate each year, the annualized dividend of your Cisco share in 2028 is $3.30. Your dividend payment from that one share of Cisco more than doubled and you didn't even buy another share.

An annualized dividend of $1.40 per share for a $45 stock is a 3.11% yield. Now that you're getting an annualized dividend of $3.30 in this example, you now have a 7.33% dividend yield without doing anything extra.

$1.40 / 45 = 3.11% dividend yield
$3.30 / 45 = 7.33% dividend yield

With the assumptions still in play, it would only take an additional 4 years to get a dividend yield of more than 10% from the Cisco stock you purchased in 2019.

I used Cisco in this example but that doesn't mean you should rush to buy Cisco on that alone. The company could have changed for the better or for the worse since I wrote this book.

Many investors look for stocks that offer the highest dividends. While some of these companies can be reliable, a high dividend yield can lead into a high-yield trap. When a stock loses value, the dividend yield increases because the dividend per share never changes. In the Cisco scenario, a $1.40 annualized dividend comes to a 3.11% yield when Cisco is priced at $45. However, if Cisco's price drops to $40, the yield rises to 3.5% because the $1.40 annualized dividend didn't change.

Some stocks with high dividends can have issues within the fundamental business model. Investors flee the stock which is why the yields get so high. While a broad market selloff can make dividend yields very attractive, you have to consider if one company with a high dividend yield can continue supporting the dividend.

You can just as easily invest in a reliable company with a growing dividend. Wait a few years, and you will have a reliable dividend stock with a yield over 10% rather than buying a very risky stock with a 10% yield in the moment.

At one point, GameStop had a 15% dividend yield. From 2013 to 2015 the company was able to grow its dividend nicely. The dividend went up by 20% from 2013 to 2014 and then by 9.1% from 2014 to 2015.

It became increasingly apparent that GameStop didn't fully adapt to e-commerce.

The dividend yield is just a simple math formula where you divide the annual dividend by how much you paid for the stock. For the next two years, GameStop raised its quarterly dividend by $0.01 per share which is more of a symbolic gesture to say the business model is still fine. However, once GameStop raised its quarterly dividend from $0.37 per share to $0.38 per share in 2017, the company never raised its dividend for over two years.

Then GameStop slashed their dividend entirely.

It's easy to look at a 15% yield and think it's really good money. The compounding on that would look incredible and make a retirement through dividend investing seem quick from a mathematical standpoint.

However, some high yielding stocks are ticking time bombs rather than opportunities to build up your wealth.

Dividend payments, the reinvestment of those dividend payments, appreciation, and a dividend's growth rate are the four key ways that dividend investors make money from dividend stocks. The dividend income can look small in the present but gets significantly larger as you become more patient.

Let's say you bought 1,000 shares of Cisco in 2019, keep them until 2028, and the 10% growth rate stays constant.

When you got those shares, they produced a combined annualized dividend of $1400. However, at the end of 2028, Cisco is paying you an annualized dividend of $3,300 for those same 100 shares. Your dividend income more than doubled and you didn't do anything extra.

This does not include if you reinvested the Cisco shares at which point you'd have 1,636 shares instead of your 1,000 shares. Then, instead of "only" making $3,300 each year from Cisco's dividends, you will make $5,398.80 each year from Cisco's dividend assuming you reinvest all of your shares.

In the example, 1,000 shares of Cisco cost $45,000. The $5,398.80 dividend from 2028 alone puts you in a solid position to get a positive ROI not to mention all of the other dividend payments and if Cisco stock appreciates in the real world scenario.

It's amazing how if you just give it time, the annualized dividend payment can go from $1,400 to $5,398.80 without you touching it ever again.

While appreciation is a factor in total returns, we don't include it in these calculations because it's impossible to predict the degree to which a stock will appreciate or depreciate…especially if you're looking more than a year into the future.

The Key Reason Dividend Investors Win

Dividend investors win because they buy reliable companies that offer a growing dividend and hold onto them for a long period of time. If a company's stock price declines in price, dividend investors see it as an opportunity to buy more and as a way to get more shares through the reinvestment since the reinvestment occurs at a lower share price.

I used to have a portfolio filled with growth stocks that didn't pay any dividends. It was amazing when they went up, but when these same stocks went down, I kept checking in on them and sold a bunch of them at the wrong times.

Dividend investors don't care whether the market goes up or down because they hold over the long-term. If their stock goes up in price, they win with appreciation. If the stock goes down in price, they win with the dividend reinvestment's ability to get more shares.

In the example from before, if Cisco stock goes down to $40 and stays at that level, and the dividend growth rate continues to go up by 10%, you are looking at a much higher dividend income in 2028.

If Cisco stock goes up to $50, you may be looking at a lower dividend income, but you still win with the 11.11% price appreciation which cushions the lost dividend income. While this is a minimal appreciation over 10 years, it's just an example to demonstrate you win either way.

For stocks that do not offer dividends, the only way to build your wealth is through the appreciation. The issue with relying on appreciation is that you can have a year of solid appreciation only for most or all of it to be taken down in a correction or recession.

In September 2019, Roku went from $169.86 per share to $99.74 per share. You have to be a mentally strong investor to handle that type of loss and not sell...especially if you bought at around $130 and know that you're not getting a dividend from your Roku shares. To Roku's credit, it had an upward trend on the way to recovery but didn't return to its $169.86 high in 2019.

Could Roku collapse? Maybe. Could its growth narrative continue to hold strong and give shareholders massive gains? Maybe.

Is it risky? Incredibly so...especially if Roku squares off against a down market.

Dividend stocks present a cushion during recessions as long as they can continue paying and raising the dividend. Stocks without the dividend put you back at Square 1 if they appreciate 20% and then lose all of that appreciation.

How Much Money Do You Need?

Earlier I mentioned how retiring from dividends is a math game. The more money you put into dividend stocks early, the higher your dividend income will become as you give it time to compound.

In the example I provided, we saw how Cisco could provide you with $5,398.80 each year which you will receive in quarterly payments. That averages out to $449.90 each month (quarterly payments are $1,799.60).

An extra $449.90 each month isn't enough to retire on. However, it definitely helps, especially when considering you did nothing extra other than your initial investment.

Holding onto the scenario I provided, if you bought 5,000 shares of Cisco in 2019 at $45 per share, that would have been a $225,000 investment that would now be bringing in, on average, around $2,249.50 each month with what would now be 8,180 Cisco shares because of the reinvestments ($26,994 in dividend income each year).

$26,994 in annual dividend income makes retirement look more feasible, especially if you stretch it out another 10 years where the compounding will only get stronger...or if you invest more into dividends.

If you got the 5,000 Cisco shares in 2019 and only need $2,000/mo to cover living expenses and everything else, you can retire in this scenario.

Remember that 5,000 shares of Cisco with an annualized dividend of $1.40 only gives you $7,000 each year at the start instead of the $26,994 we end up with in the scenario I provided where Cisco's dividend continues to grow at around 10% each year.

If the dividend grows by 10% for another year and you reinvest, your annual $26,994 payment turns into an annual $32,257.73 payment and you now have 8,862.014 shares instead of the 8180 shares from the prior year...with no extra work on your part.

Assuming after all of these years the shares are still at $45 (insanely big assumption in the real world but good for the example), those 8,862.014 shares are now worth $398,790.63 which is a 77.24% increase from the initial $245,000 investment.

Each year, your dividend income will grow more than the year before. You will have to look at your tax laws to see how much of that dividend income you get to keep. The rules vary from state to state.

How Do We Get That $245,000?

In the example where the numbers get really big, the portfolio starts off with 5,000 Cisco shares at $45 each which came to

$245,000. This scenario works out great as you get paid $26,994 in dividends every year.

However, this scenario also assumes you have $245,000 in hand and ready to go…and most of us don't fit into that category. This is why we started this book off by sharing how you build up your financial discipline so you invest in your future rather than spend your money on stuff that you'll forget about later.

Financial discipline itself won't get you the $245,000 you're looking for in this example, but it will help you better utilize the money you currently earn. Some people make $300,000 every year only to spend $400,000 of it on mostly unnecessary and over-the-top expenses.

This is why it is better to invest when you are young. Granted, if you don't fall into that category, you should not use timing as an excuse. Rather, you should look to boost your earned income so you have more money to invest in dividend stocks and other investment vehicles if you choose to go into multiple directions.

Unless you win the lottery and use those winnings smartly or make 7-figures each year, you won't suddenly have $245,000 available that you can just pour into various dividend stocks. However, you have time.

Rather than think of it was $245,000, think of it as monthly payments. Right now, I invest $2,000 every month into dividend stocks. Since reliable companies that provide dividends are good to own in good times and bad times, I have no problem with a monthly investment.

That monthly investment also happens during those bad times which means I get stocks at discounts when the prices go down. $2,000 each month adds up to $24,000 every year. At this rate, it will take a little over 10 years to reach $245,000 in invested capital.

However, it won't take as long for you to reach $245,000 if you invest $2,000 each month. Each $2,000 investment is going towards dividend stocks that give you a dividend. Let's say you invest in stocks that, on average, have a 3% yield at the time of purchase and a 10% dividend growth rate.

Each $2,000/mo investment gives you an extra $60/yr in dividends that will grow by 10% each year. For a single $2,000 investment, we are looking at a dividend of $155.62/yr without reinvesting the dividend or doing extra work. If you make a monthly $2,000 investment into dividend stocks, you'll get 12 of those $155.62 dividend payments at the end of Year 10 for total of $1,867.44 each year. While I'd never count the dividend reinvestments in this way, they could eventually cover a month of investing $2,000 if you give them time to grow.

This does not include reinvesting the dividends, and with Years 2-9 to invest dividends before you reach Year 10, you'll be making much more than $1,867.44 each year by the time it's all said and done.

If you do not have $2,000 you can invest each month, start with what you can invest each month. Building up your financial discipline and living a frugal lifestyle will help you make better use of your earned income. Again, even if you can't invest much, a single penny gets you in the game. While the penny is more symbolic than anything else, it gets you started.

You can also get a free stock using Rohinhood. I'll put the link here one more time: join.robinhood.com/marcg665.

With that said, I believe most people can find $100/mo to invest in dividend stocks. Cutting down on some expenses is one way to reach this milestone. Selling items around the house is another way to achieve this goal. You can also do a side hustle that brings in an extra $100 each month, and rather than view it as extra spending money, view it as extra investing money.

I know each person's financial situation is different. Some people have no problem investing $10,000 each month into dividend stocks while others have to scramble to find an extra $100 to invest in dividend stocks each month. Regardless of where you are, the most important thing to do is start. The hardest part of this entire process is starting. As you get deeper into the process and make the consistent monthly investments, your portfolio will expand and so will your dividend income.

Why You Need A Monthly Investment Goal

$2,000/mo is the investment goal I currently have that helps me build up my dividend investing portfolio. Eventually I will raise this goal but for now $2,000/mo is the goal. You should think of raising your goal in the future because if you're not growing you're dying.

A monthly investment goal is critical for any dividend investor because the goal is close enough to notice but not too close to the point of overwhelm. Some people can set a week-ly investment goal, but for other people it may be stressful to keep up with that type of goal.

And if you miss the weekly goal once, it can create a negative snowball effect. A month gives you more time but not too much time. You'll stay focused on the goal and continue to think about how you spend each dollar. If you invest once every quarter, that's more time for tempting purchases to pull money out of your wallet and leave you short of your goal.

Monthly investments also allow you to balance the good times and bad times of the economy. If you invest $2,000 during a market high and the market goes down by 10%, then your next $2,000 investment will happen during the market correction which will help your cost basis (i.e. instead of a 10% loss, we're only talking about a 5% loss because that's the average of 0% and a 10% loss over two months).

Know Your Retirement Gap

The retirement gap is the difference between how much mon-ey you need to make each year to retire and how much mon-ey you currently make from your dividend stocks and other investment vehicles each year.

You can reduce the gap by decreasing how much money you need at retirement and by investing more money into dividend stocks. For those who invest, time does the most work to cut down on the gap.

Earlier I mentioned $245,000 in my example. That may be more or less than what you actually need to retire on dividend investing. The more money you invest each month, the sooner you will completely close the gap.

There are some variables you can't account for such as the movement of a stock's price which will affect how many shares your money can purchase. The dividend growth rate is another key variable that you don't have any control over. All you can control is how much money you invest each month and the research you do so you end up with the right dividend stocks.

One common mistake people make with dividend investing is they only think in terms of the yield and what you'd get now if you invest X amount of dollars. If you need to make $5,000 each month from your dividend income to retire ($60,000 each year), you don't have to wait until you can invest $2 million in dividend stocks that average a 3% yield.

You continue investing month after month and wait for the reinvestments and dividend growth to take effect.

Part 3

Increasing Your Earned Income

Your profit determines how much you can invest into dividend stocks and other investment vehicles. Increasing your earned income increases your potential profit. As long as your spending doesn't rise each time you increase your earned income, your profit will grow.

We have already talked about developing financial discipline for your current income and expenses. However, we will now talk about some of the ways you can increase your earned income.

For the most part, a job presents very few opportunities for earned income growth. You can move up to a higher position or ask for a raise, but these types of movements don't happen often. Many people advise not asking for a raise more than once a year. Even then, these pay raises aren't likely to provide a dramatic boost to your earned income.

You can be a valuable member of the organization, but that doesn't necessarily guarantee you move up the ladder quicker. With that said, there is no cap to the amount of earned income you can make if you start a business. You don't need to hire anyone to start your business and it can be entirely based on what you enjoy doing.

Businesses take time to develop, but once they are developed and you know how to scale, you can increase your earned income and eventually have the earned income from your business ventures surpass the earned income from your job.

On the first episode of the Ditch The Job Podcast, I interviewed Tamara Patzer who ditched her job and proceeded to triple her income with her own business.

Like many people, she was physically and emotionally worn out from her job and the long commute. Instead of accepting this as her life, she found time in her schedule to educate herself. She listened to cassettes and DVDs during her commutes. Today, we can more easily tap into educational content through audiobooks and podcast episodes.

She built up her mindset and built relationships with business owners who eventually became her clients. She used her money from the job to eventually leave her job behind for her new business.

It takes time to build up this type of earned income. Just like anything else in life, you have to make sacrifices. Tamara was smart with her money and that's what allowed her to build up her income and ditch her job.

The great thing about receiving earned income from a business is that you can actively put in the work to boost it. If you make $100 for every podcast episode you publish, you can produce more podcast episodes and launch more podcasts.

This is why I currently host three podcasts. I love the business model and it allows me to grow my revenue. By keeping expenses at bay, I also expand my profit. This expanded profit gives me more money to invest into dividend stocks.

I can run more Amazon Ads and write more books to boost my book royalties. I can also promote my coaching and courses to make more revenue.

The key difference between a job and a business is that with a business there's always something you can do to boost your earned income. At a job, you have a set earned income and it doesn't matter how productive you are. For the most part, your earned income is going to stay the same, and you can get penalized if you are not productive enough and do not meet certain criteria.

Plus, at a job, if that's your only source of income, you're in a ton of financial trouble if the company hiring you decides to downsize or fires you. Having multiple streams of income as a business owner and investor lessens the blow if one of those streams dries up.

There are a variety of ways to increase your earned income. Some tactics are easy and don't require too much effort. Online surveys fit into this category. While you can make some quick money, filling out online surveys won't provide the sustainable level of income you can use to ditch your job or make massive monthly investments into your dividend portfolio.

There are other strategies to boosting your earned income that involve more work and can take several months or even years to see the payoff. However, the payoff is massive once you reach it.

The foundation behind any business is that you provide value that attracts a certain type of person who is willing to pay you for a product or service.

Here are some ways you can provide a level of value that would be met with prospects inquiring about your services.

Podcasting — this is by far my favorite business model. You interview at least one guest for your show each week. Not only does this give you more content to share with your audience, but some of the guests end up becoming clients if you position yourself well and build the relationship over time.

Self-Publishing Books — many people dream of writing their own book and yet only a few people do. Self-publishing books is a great opportunity to earn additional income that can turn into full-time income. Some authors make their full-time income from the book royalties alone but most authors turn their books into full-time income machines by leveraging their books to get more clients and get on more stages. If writing a book intimidates you, start with a journal. These are ridiculously easy to create (many journals are simply the same page repeated 90 or more times).

Blogging and Vlogging — Both of these platforms present you with the opportunity to give your audience free content. This will build up the relationship between you and your audience. Some people in your audience may decide to buy the product or service you are offering.

Affiliate Marketing — don't have a product or service yet? No problem. Promote someone else's product or service and earn a commission for each sale you make. Amazon's affiliate program starts at a 4% commission for most items and some affiliate programs give you as much as a 50% commission on each sale if you sell their stuff.

Training Courses — Create a bunch of videos around the same topic and turn it into a training course people pay to get access to. You can promote your training course in your free content and to your email list (most important asset of any online business). If you are camera shy, you can start by recording slideshow presentations using a software like ScreenFlow or Camtasia.

Freelancing — Certain websites like UpWork and Fiverr are great places for freelancers to earn extra money during their spare time. You can perform a variety of tasks on these sites such as social media management, writing articles, being a virtual assistant, and many more. While it's common to find people who will charge low prices for their services on these sites, it is possible to build up a respectable amount of income. Some people make full-time incomes with UpWork and/or Fiverr but you'll find more people making full-time income with the previously mentioned methods.

The Gig Economy — The gig economy is fully in effect and businesses like Uber and AirBnB present great opportunities to boost your earned income. This method of boosting your earned income isn't for everyone but both of these resources will build up your income and allow you to meet a bunch of new people. While trying to offer your products or services to these people can result in bad reviews, you can tell them about your brand and build a relationship.

Pro Tip: The next time you order an Uber or Lyft, tell the driver about what you do. You might get a new podcast listener, YouTube subscriber, or blog visitor depending on which one you promote. Get comfortable promoting yourself.

Coaching — This is one of my favorite monetization models because you get to impact people in a big way. In a coaching experience, you get to know your client on a deeper level and watch them grow in real-time. Coaching is highly rewarding when you see your clients become successful and it pays well. Nowadays my primary self-education strategy is to hire coaches who have mastered the skills I want to develop. Kindle Unlimited, SkillShare, and the library of books I've bought over the years cover the rest.

Pro Tip: Kindle Unlimited and SkillShare both offer free trials so you can get used to their platforms. This is a great opportunity to learn new skills for free and invest in them if it's the right fit. I have provided the links below for anyone who is interested.

I do receive some compensation if you join through those links. However, I speak as someone who currently invests in both Kindle Unlimited and SkillShare for my continued education.

Get 30 free days of Kindle Unlimited: https://amzn.to/35b5wFM

Get 2 free months of SkillShare: https://skl.sh/2QbZgt9

Done For You Services — Some people won't want to do certain tasks. They would rather hand that work off to someone else and pay that person for doing the work. This is where you come in. Social media marketing, book writing, and podcast launches are some of the many done for you services that are offered nowadays. You can create a done for you service around your expertise and start reaching out to people who could benefit from your services.

Sponsorships — While this is a monetization method better suited for people with decent sized audiences, it is an income stream to think about. I podcasted for over two years before I began making money from sponsorships, but once I tapped into this income stream, the revenue rose quickly. Sponsorships are currently one of my top income streams and there are a variety of ways to expand this income stream as you grow audiences on different platforms.

Those are 10 of the top ways to build up your earned income that don't involve you starting a job. If you are employed, think of how you can find time in your day to build up these income streams and if any colleagues can help you grow your audience or become potential clients.

Some people prefer to view their jobs as places they despise without thinking of the opportunities that are right in front of them. The cultures of any workplace vary greatly, but if you see the opportunities rather than the parts you don't like, you can get out of your job sooner if that's the path you want to take.

One of the most common mistakes people make is going all-in on all of these income streams. The problem with approaching all of these income streams is that you spread yourself too thin. It is better to pick a few to start with and have them complement each other.

Use your podcast as a medium to promote your coaching and done for your services to your listeners and guests. If you also want to self-publish books, make sure you mention your podcast in each of your books. The more you can connect these income streams, the more repeat business you will get.

There are several side hustles that let you make a few extra hundred dollars each month with some creating the potential for thousands of dollars each month if you heavily invest your time into them. However, I preferred to share the streams of income that can quickly add up and represent a full-time income.

Uber and AirBnB are the only ones on the list I have not tried at some point. AirBnB has more potential as you leverage your home and can use the AirBnB revenue to pay off your mortgage and other living expenses. Granted, you still have to attract people to your location by ranking well on AirBnB and being a courteous host, but AirBnB makes house hacking easier for anyone to utilize.

For people who don't know, house hacking is when you buy a multi-family property, live in one unit, and rent out the other unit. Therefore, the person in the other unit effectively pays your mortgage and other expenses on the property. This type of living arrangement makes it easier for a dividend investor to build up their portfolio and compound more of their dividend income sooner.

Finding Time For The Other Streams Of Earned Income
The more streams of earned income you have, the more you can weather a sudden change around one of those income streams. I've had income streams dry up in the past, but I didn't feel the impact because my other income streams grew to make up for the deficiency.

The more time you find to boost your earned income, the better your chances are to see significant results in boosting your earned income. My recommendation is to start with 1-3 of these income streams and build from there when you know what you are doing.

The best way to address the required work to create those new streams of income is to put them in your schedule. Each day, have a set time of day to work on one of your earned income streams. Then, set a different time of day to work on an additional earned income stream.

Giving yourself a set time to perform tasks around a certain theme gives you clarity on what to do next. The reason people don't feel like they have enough time to do various things is because they don't have a schedule in place.

There are certain things I don't have enough time to do for the sole reason that they aren't priorities and I'm okay with not doing them. However, I don't catch myself saying the same thing about priorities. I put priorities on the schedule and all of the other tasks throughout the day are framed around the times that I've set for priorities.

I like to accomplish all of the 3-4 key priorities of the day before addressing any other part of my business. Every day I wake up and pursue Priority #1. For me, that's usually writing content for my latest book. I have many more books in the pipeline after this book and plan on doubling my total number of books from 25 to 50 in 2020…so watch this space (that doubling does not include no content books like journals which are ridiculously easy to write).

By starting the day on a key priority, it allows me to stay focused throughout the day. On days where I started the day by going on social media or doing something unproductive, those distractions had a stronger presence for the entire day. When you focus on priorities first, it is easier to resist anything that does not align with your priorities.

One of the biggest lies people come up with is saying they don't have enough time. It all boils down to mindset and how you will allocate your time once you know what your true priorities are. There is a difference between being busy and being productive. One of the items on my list is to post something on Facebook. Posting on social media allows me to better connect with my audience and let them know what I am doing.

However, social media isn't something that has to get my attention at the beginning of the day when I am at my peak. The beginning of the day is for book writing or any other key priority. The Facebook post can wait until the afternoon or evening when my productivity lags anyway.

The danger of me posting on Facebook in the morning is that I may browse through Facebook and suddenly realize I've been on the site for 30 minutes. Social networks are very good at keeping our attention and presenting us with content that we want to see and consume.

If you have a job, wake up 30 minutes earlier so you can accomplish or at least start working on one of your priorities before the commute and job kick in. Use some of your lunch break to build up your podcast, write your next book, create videos for your training course, or anything else that will help you boost your earned income.

Boosting Your Productivity

Committing time to build up streams of earned income is a terrific starting point. The next step is to boost your productivity. To demonstrate, consider the act of writing a book. Most people type at a speed of around 40 words per minute.

Because I have written enough books and blog posts, I can get to around 80 words per minute when the ideas are flowing. 80 WPM is twice the productivity of 40 WPM from an output standpoint. In an hour, 40 WPM gets you 2,400 words while 80 WPM gets you 4,800 words.

I almost never write 4,800 words in an hour because you have to continuously think of ideas and not get distracted for that entire hour. However, it makes it much easier for me to write 3,000 words in an hour. This comes with practice.

One area where you can create more content is by talking it out. While the average person types at around 40 words per minute, the average person can speak at a rate of 125-150 words per minute which is more than three times the rate in which the average person writes content.

I personally prefer to write content than talk it, but if you can talk your content, you'll boost your productivity.

Boosting your productivity all comes down to achieving the same output in a shorter amount of time. Part of boosting your productivity is working faster so you can increase your output in a shorter amount of time.

Boosting your productivity also involves optimizing your body and work schedule for success. Your energy is a key determinant in how productive you are throughout the day. Getting the proper amount of sleep, exercising at some point, and eating healthy are three key factors in boosting your energy.

You should get at least 7 hours of sleep and look to build up to 8 hours of sleep each day if you are not there already. On some days, you should avoid setting an alarm and let your body naturally wake up. The risk with setting an alarm is that it can go off in the middle of your sleep cycle while you can naturally complete your sleep cycle if you do not use the alarm.

You need an alarm if you have to be somewhere at a certain time, but when that is not the case, make it a point to wake up naturally.

There are many factors that go into healthy living. You may want to consider picking up a copy of Healthy Living Every Day which is available on Amazon. My mom wrote the book and it contains practical advice for each day of the year to boost your health.

Daily exercise will also help with your productivity, but the exercise doesn't have to be strenuous. I run every day because that is the path I have chosen, and I want to run as many marathons as I can.

A simple 5-10 minute stretching routine also fires up the endorphins which will help with your productivity and self-confidence. These are the things you do outside of your work that allow you to be more focused and committed when you work on what needs to get done.

Boosting your productivity also involves optimizing your work schedule. I briefly touched on this earlier when mentioning that you want to address key priorities first and address your lower level tasks later in the day. Optimizing your work schedule also means working at times when you are at your highest level of productivity.

You can reach your highest level of productivity when you have no distractions around you and no one to talk to. The only exception to the latter is if the work you're doing is cooperative in which you have your working buddies with you but no one else.

Being in this state allows you to more easily tap into the flow. The sooner you get into the flow, the quicker the minutes will seem to fly. If you've ever looked back and were amazed at how much you did within 30 minutes, you were in the flow. Getting into your flow more often and extending the amount of time you spend in your flow will greatly enhance your productivity and move you closer to your goals.

When you are in a state of flow but know you'll have to depart from that state of flow soon, write some of your current thoughts down so you can quickly return back to your flow. When I have to take a break from writing books, I jot down the next few thoughts I wanted to cover and always end each writing session with an incomplete sentence.

Finishing that incomplete sentence allows me to start the writing session with action rather than thinking of what I'm supposed to do next. Since this more quickly puts me in the state of writing, I have an easier time addressing the thoughts I jotted down from the previous writing session.

You may not pursue book writing as your extra source of earned income, but if you can write down your thoughts before you leave your flow and end with an incomplete thought, it will be easier for you to get back into the flow the next time you work.

Live Like You Are Not Making The Extra Income

All of the extra earned income should go towards investing in your future. Earning extra income doesn't mean you should expand your lifestyle.

By not expanding your lifestyle in proportion to your expanded earnings, you'll have far more money to invest into dividend stocks and reap dramatically higher returns over the long-term.

You should try to live on 20% of your earned income. If you make $100,000 every year, you should live like you only make $20,000/yr. This will give you a lot of extra money to invest and allow you to make smarter decisions with your money.

The extra income is a way to achieve financial freedom sooner and set up future generations for financial freedom. Think of what the dividend income will look like at Year 50 assuming a modest growth rate (going that far into the future requires a modest growth rate of around 5% because a company will have likely matured by then. Dividend stocks are only buy and hold forever stocks if the company continues to look strong, so don't assume you have to hold onto the same stocks for 50+ years).

Part of the goal behind pursuing side hustles and building some of them into businesses is to increase how much money you can invest into dividend stocks each month. Each extra dollar you invest can earn itself back and much more the earlier you invest that extra dollar.

The idea behind this approach is to delay your gratification. Instant gratification attracts us to the wrong decisions and habits. It's patience and waiting for the long-term payoff that results in financial freedom and goal achievement.

Part 4

Deciding Which Dividend Stocks To Buy

Now comes the important part…deciding which dividend stocks you will add to your portfolio. You could have the right mindset for boosting your earned income, spending as little of it as possible, and investing the rest into dividend stocks and other investment vehicles.

However, the stocks you pick determine what type of return you will get. Before we go any further, it is essential for you determine what criteria you look for in a dividend stock.

A criteria is a set of rules you use to determine if a stock should be added to your portfolio. If you don't have a set criteria, the risk is that you chase stocks that have had a strong return in the past year only for the stock to run out of luck when you decide to buy shares in that company.

Setting a criteria eliminates other options that could distract you from pursuing the portfolio that makes the most sense for you.

If your criteria is set to only invest in dividend stocks, then you've already eliminated a bunch of companies. This is good because you get to focus in on a few companies which allows you to specialize in a narrow category rather than having decent knowledge of a broad category.

You can go deeper into the dividend stock categorization. You can solely focus on companies with a high dividend growth rate or companies that currently offer a high dividend yield with a lower dividend growth rate.

I personally like dividend stocks yielding 3% with around a 6-10% annual dividend growth rate. Sometimes I'll buy a stock that offers a 2.5% dividend yield but a 20% annual dividend growth rate. At other times, I'll buy a stock that offers a 5% dividend yield with a 4% annual dividend growth rate.

You can make some slight compromises to the model if it means getting shares in a company you believe will be valuable in the long-term and caters to your current needs. Some dividend investors have a stronger desire to boost their current dividend income. Others are willing to take the lower dividend yield now and wait for it to build up over time.

You can also invest in REITs (real estate investment trusts) which tend to offer higher dividend yields (they are required to pay 90% of their taxable income as unqualified dividend income). However, dividends from REITs are treated as ordinary income which means they get taxed at a higher rate than dividend income. Hence they fall into the unqualified dividend income category.

You can find some REITs that pay dividends at around 8-12% depending on where you look. Most of these kinds of REITs will be Mortgage REITs.

For REITs, the biggest thing to focus on other than the economy is the interest rate. If the interest rate decreases, bonds are less attractive which will cause some investors flock over to REITs. Lower interest rates also decreases the cost for REITs to borrow money for their real estate investments. Higher interest rates increase the cost of borrowing and make bonds more attractive.

The lower the interest rates, the better REITs generally tend to perform. You still have to check fundamentals to make sure a certain REIT is a good investment.

In any event, you should have an idea of what you are after as a dividend investor. Do you want the high yield, the high dividend growth rate, or a middle ground that gives you both but on lower scales?

Here are some other areas to consider when shaping your criteria. You can use some, all, or none of these factors to create your criteria.

Financials — I primarily invest in profitable companies. These are the types of companies that can continue offering reliable dividends. Some people go after growth companies that sacrifice profit for several years and rely on debt for growth. Sometimes this works wonderfully. At other times your investment can crash spectacularly. You can also look at changes in profit margin and debt to shape your criteria.

Sectors — A good investor diversifies across many sectors. If you only invest in REITs, your portfolio is made or broken by how interest rates move. Other factors matter, but the interest rate would have too much of an influence on your portfolio.

This is why investors diversify. Here is a list of the different sectors you can choose from:

Information Technology — XLK

Energy — XLE

Industrials — XLI

Real Estate — XLRE

Consumer Staples — XLP

Consumer Discretionary — XLY

Basic Materials — XLB

Financial — XLF

Healthcare — XLV

Utilities — XLU

Communications — XTL

The tickers are the ETFs for each category. That way if you want to dive into financials and invest in specific companies, but you don't want to do the same for basic materials or another sector, you can invest in XLB instead of doing the research on basic materials companies.

You do not have to invest in all of these ETFs or individual sectors. I prefer to buy shares of an S&P 500 index fund to have full diversification instead of investing into ETFs of individual sectors.

That way, I can specialize in fewer sectors and know which companies to invest in. Since I only focus on a few sectors and already have a criteria for the type of dividend stocks fit my portfolio, I can quickly trim down the potential list of stocks.

Do Your Research Before Buying

You should never buy a dividend stock after looking at it for just a few minutes. Before you buy a stock, you should always conduct research which comes in two parts. The first part is checking off the items on your criteria and looking at a company's financials.

You can easily look at a company's financials through Yahoo! Finance (free resource) or by going through a company's 10-K. If you want to go the 10-K route which is more detailed but offers more context than you can get from Yahoo! Finance, search for the investor relations for that company.

For instance, if you want to find the investor relations of Cisco, search "Cisco Investor Relations" in a search engine like Google and you'll find Cisco's 10-K and other important documents.

The second part of your research is public sentiment. While public sentiment can't be measured, it plays a vital role in a stock's valuation. It is important to look at financials first because the public and the media can get it wrong.

To see people and the media continue to get proper valuations wrong, look no further than Bitcoin. While I personally do not recommend Bitcoin, some people love it and feel confident about its future.

The point I am trying to make is that people's thoughts on Bitcoin's price vary greatly. Venture capitalist Tim Draper claimed that BTC/USD could reach $250,000 as soon as the end of 2020.

Meanwhile, a Forbes article details how Bitcoin could fall below $6,000.

A few years from now, one of these claims is going to be spectacularly wrong. Could Bitcoin fall below $6,000 and then rise up to $250,000. Technically it's possible, but it's also technically possible for any investment vehicle to make that type of gain if there is enough demand.

On a side note, it's crazy to think some people and websites are already giving predictions for what Bitcoin's price will be in 2030...before we even got started with the 2020s.

If you rely on people's opinions and the media, you risk coming up with false conclusions and making investments based on those false conclusions. People's opinions and the media are great for determining the public sentiment around the investment you're looking at.

Know what your opinion is going into the investment, follow smart investors and see what they're saying, listen to other people and the media, and with all of that information...make a decision and act on it.

When Schwab and TD Ameritrade announced zero fees on stock trades, public sentiment was that these brokerage companies did a ton of damage to their bottom lines and both companies dropped by over 20% in a few days.

A closer look at financials revealed that the drop was warranted but was exaggerated. This presented a buying opportunity. Sure enough, the stocks of both companies bounced back quickly as people paid more attention to the financials than the media hype.

More people realized that zero fees on stock trades wasn't as devastating as previously thought. Schwab buying TD Ameritrade sent both share prices higher and well past their price points before the news broke out about zero fees on stock trades.

Public sentiment shouldn't guide your decisions. It's just a way to see how the public currently views a company and if a buying opportunity exists.

A lot of people who loved Bitcoin in 2017 weren't loving it as much in 2018. Time will tell for Bitcoin. The same can be said about every investment vehicle. I only bring up Bitcoin because it has a wide range of public opinions and extreme price movements. If you want to see how public sentiment alone can move an investment vehicle, look no further than Bitcoin, especially in the years 2017 and 2018.

You can also look at the tulip mania back in the 17th century to see public sentiment in action. Before the tulip collapse, the average price of a single flower surpassed annual incomes of skilled workers and house prices. Then the prices quickly plummeted over a week. It is considered the first financial bubble.

Changing Up Your Portfolio

It is not good to change your portfolio too much, but keeping your portfolio the same can expose you to some risks. One risk is that you realize you leaned too heavily into a certain sector and want to diversify.

Another reason to change up your portfolio is because you find companies that better fit your criteria than one of the companies you currently invest in. When investors can't find great deals that perfectly match their criteria, they adjust their criteria for the sake of making more investments in companies that are similar but not perfect criteria fits.

This is similar to how I mentioned I'll buy a company with a 2.5% yield but currently has a 20% annual dividend growth rate even though I prefer 3% yields. If I suddenly find a company with a 3.1% yield with the same annual dividend growth rate, and the fundamentals of both companies are similar, I'm shifting some of my funds from the 2.5% yield company to the 3.1% yield company.

Stocks can also fall out of favor based on how the companies change. Dividend growth rates typically stall as the company gets more mature. If the dividend growth rate falls under 5%, it's enough cause of concern for me to look at other companies and consider moving some of my funds.

Just because a stock fits into your criteria when you buy it does not mean that same stock will fit into your criteria years later.

Changing up your portfolio also prevents you from over-weighting certain stocks. Before I took the dividend approach, there was a time when Amazon made up 50% of my portfolio. This was not a smart decision as my returns for the day, week, and month revolved around what Amazon did.

I had no coverage when Amazon went down and no dividends on the way.

Today I still have some Amazon shares and it's one of the few stocks I own that doesn't offer a dividend. However, it's nowhere near 50% of my portfolio. Today Amazon makes up less than 10% of my portfolio. The same can be said about most of the stocks in my portfolio. I have some stocks that make up more than 10% of my portfolio (these are all dividend stocks), but none surpass 20% of my portfolio's total value.

If a stock surpasses 20% of your portfolio's value, it's time to look around for other options so your returns aren't overly dependent on one company's success or failure.

While it is good to change some parts of your portfolio, it's also important to weigh different options before making any changes. If you sell shares at a gain, you will have to pay capital gains. If you held onto the shares for less than a year and then sold them, you'll have to pay more in capital gains.

If you sell shares at a loss, you can use the losses as a tax write off against your gains. Some investors choose to keep their dividend shares at a loss because that means the reinvested dividend gets you more shares.

In the long-term, holding onto a beat up dividend stock can give you plenty of extra shares that continue bringing in more dividend income. Holding onto a beat up dividend stock only becomes a problem when the fundamentals fall apart similar to the GE scenario.

With that in mind, you should never buy or sell a dividend stock just based on a headline. Even with the approach from before, it's easy for people to fall prey to emotionally grabbing headlines.

It's easy to hear about a stock that jumped 20% in one week and "has more room to run" and abandon your existing strategy. When you chase these sensational headlines without knowing the fundamentals, you're gambling and hoping for the best. This is where public sentiment can steer you in the wrong direction.

While dividend investing is a path to consistent, predictable, and growing income that you do a little work to build up, it is not your full-time work. If you invest in stocks based on sensational headlines, you will keep monitoring your shares multiple times throughout the day to see how they are doing.

This constant monitoring will take you away from building up your earned income which will help you invest more money and cover living expenses.

I know that's true because that's what happened to me in my early stages when I just looked for the headlines and relied too much on public sentiment.

Dividend investing takes a more passive approach after you purchase the shares. I could go a week without logging into Fidelity and be emotionally fine. If you buy based on sensational headlines on the hopes the stock still has more room to run and can give you a 20% return too, you may end up checking your brokerage account every hour.

Unless you work at Wall Street, you shouldn't be looking at your investments every hour. Investing allows you to take your money and put it into stocks or other investment vehicles that build your wealth.

In the short-term, you don't get paid to invest unless that's what your job is. Investing pays off in the long-term, but you still need to do things to build up your portfolio.

It's good to change up parts of your portfolio 1-2 times each quarter. However, it's not good to check your portfolio and make too many trades. From an ROI standpoint, it is better to buy and hold reliable companies than it is to day trade.

There could be outliers, but for the most part, people who buy and hold tend to get higher returns than day traders.

Is Cash Ever King?

When you invest in a dividend stock, you allocate cash towards that specific asset. You can't spend $1,000 on Cisco stock and then use that same money to buy JPM stock.

If the company you invest in goes down by 10% momentarily, you don't get a do over. You have that 10% loss that only materializes into a write off and true loss if you sell that stock.

It doesn't always make sense to sell a stock when it goes down by 10%. Sometimes, these same stocks rally back to their highs if you give them time.

But in the moment it's tempting to let emotions win out against logic and make the decision to sell.

And in the middle of a recession, everyone seems to be selling.

This brings us to a question about cash. Is cash ever king?

The money you put into a savings account is guaranteed to lose value each year based on inflation. You could buy U.S. Treasury bonds to cut down on risk and get a low return that either barely beats inflation or at least cushions the blow.

However, we run into the similar issue that the $1,000 invested in U.S. Treasury bonds can't be used to buy $1,000 worth of JPM shares.

So does it ever make sense to just hold onto cash? This is where your research matters.

Recessions can feel like they happened overnight, but there are indicators you can use to determine if the economy is in trouble. The most popular indicator is an inverted yield curve when comparing 2 year note yields and 10 year note yields.

According to Reuters, the U.S. curve has inverted before each recession for the past 50 years and only offered one false signal during that timeframe. An inverted yield curve indicates that a recession is about 1-2 years away.

Then you look at parts of the economy like manufacturing and job growth and pay attention to how other economies are doing.

Since the world economy is very connected, if one country enters a recession, several others get hurt. Depending on which countries enter recessions, other countries can fall into recessions as well rather than getting hurt a little bit and shaking off the damage in a few months.

If you believe a recession is on the way and stocks are overvalued, look for value opportunities rather than avoid investing all together.

Timing The Market Is A Bad Long-Term Strategy

I would never tell anyone to stop investing all together. If you stop investing, you stop growing.

And if you invest in reliable companies, a recession won't matter because you'll just hold onto your shares and wait for them to go back up to pre-recession valuations.

All the while getting more shares through dividend reinvestments and continuing to invest your own money to get additional shares. A recession is actually a terrific buying opportunity if you have cash left aside. This is a scenario where cash is king.

Another scenario is if the company you're looking at faces headwinds and has a bad short-term outlook. You can wait for some of the dust to settle and invest in the company at a lower price point. Some headwinds are big "Stay Away" signs but other headwinds are temporary or cyclical.

In the temporary and cyclical scenarios, wait for the stock to get beat up a bit and then start buying. When you buy a stock at a lower price point, you get more shares with the same dollars.

Timing the market can occasionally work, but it shouldn't be the foundation of your investing strategy. The truth about the market is that we don't have any idea where it will head. Even if you think you have an idea of where it's heading, a critical piece of information can suddenly become available and dramatically change the outlook for an individual company or the entire market as a whole.

At one point, Enron's financials indicated a positive outlook and continued growth. At Enron's peak, it was the 7th largest publicly traded company.

Then came the information…and the truth. Enron was cooking the books, lying to the public, and in deep trouble.

Enron is the most commonly referenced company in many classes and textbooks.

During Enron's decline, there were still some days when the stock shot upward. Some notable upward trends are indicated by the arrows.

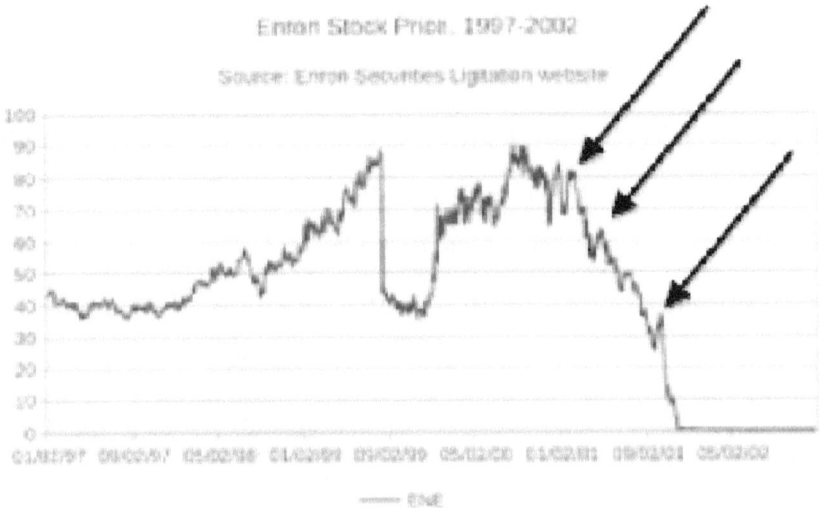

There are a few scenarios that explain the upticks:

#1: Investors at the time may have thought that the Enron case was overblown or a sham. This is more understandable in the moment and caters to the idea of buy when others are fearful. It did take several years for justice to prevail so people could have had their doubts during the process. If those investors knew what we know now, none of them would have bought Enron, but some saw the drop as temporary and thought it was a great buying opportunity. Who could blame them? Enron was #1 on *Fortune's* Most Admired Companies

Survey for 6 straight years. Even in 2001, a Goldman analyst referred to Enron as an extraordinary and unique business. There were still reasons to buy and hold Enron before the entire truth came out.

#2: Investors tried to time the market. Enron's fraudulent financials looked good before they got completely exposed. When some investors jump in and buy shares of a company, other investors may also jump in just because some people jumped in before them. For instance, if a stock goes up by 3% and there's still time left to trade, some investors may buy into that stock solely because it went up by 3% so far and they think they'll make additional gains tomorrow just because of the 3% boost. Correlation does not equal causation, but some investors don't care about that principle in the moment.

The former is based on a planned approach where you have an opinion and act based on that opinion. The latter is hoping the stock chart goes the way you want it to go for a few days before selling.

Finding the buying opportunity is saying that the stock is currently at a very low price and you should buy it right then and there. Timing the market is saying the stock is at an okay price, but I think it can go lower so I'll wait it out and see if it hits the price I want it to hit.

That's why timing the market sometimes work. You'll feel great if the stock goes down to your set price level, but you won't feel so good if the stock rises and continues to gain upward momentum.

Timing the market creates a follow the herd mentality which can put you in the trap of not thinking for yourself. See that something's going up and only buying it because other people are buying it and moving up the price. That's following the herd.

Following the herd also includes selling when everyone else sells. This is why we've got the sage Buffett advice of being greedy when others are fearful and fearful when others are greedy.

If you decide to time some investments, it is good to have some back-ups in case the timing doesn't work. I do not recommend trying to time the market at all times. Sometimes it makes sense. If stocks are all at their all-time highs, a correction should be due at some point. However, it's not something you should rely on.

Enron may be an exaggerated example, but it shows how timing the market can have bad consequences especially if you look at the chart rather than the fundamentals. It also goes to show how much a company outlook can change in a single day.

Just invest in dividend stocks, reinvest the dividends, pay attention to dividend growth rates, and watch your dividend income grow. As long as you invest in reliable companies, you'll have an easier time sleeping each night.

The Enron debacle is also a great case study for diversification. Many hard working Enron employees who didn't know about the corruption at the top invested exclusively in Enron stock for their retirement plans. Those retirement plans got wiped out in a few years.

The Enron debacle shows that you should diversify instead of relying on 1-5 stocks and thinking they'll lead you to where you want to go.

Timing the market is also bad because even if you know certain things will happen, you can miss out on great upside leading up to the events you're fearful of. For instance, the yield curve between 10 year notes and 2 year notes inverted in August 2019.

At the time of writing towards the end of December 2019, the S&P 500 is up around 10% since the yield curve inverted.

As mentioned earlier, the yield curve is an indicator that a recession could be on its way, and it's been a mostly accurate metric. However, if you pulled out upon heading about the inversion, you would have missed a 10% gain in the economy.

I can't say how an individual stock would have performed because I'd have to know which one we are talking about, but the economy has still been going up.

Could there be a recession in 2020, 2021, or another year? Maybe…maybe not. A recession is bound to happen eventually, but no one really knows when it's going to happen until it actually happens.

Of course, people can and will claim they knew all along when a recession does hit, or they'll keep saying, "Recession!" until the recession hits and take credit for it. But no one really knows when a recession or other big economic events will happen or how they will impact certain companies.

People who pulled out to time the market and hope for a recession so they could buy stocks at a discount have so far been left disappointed. Even if stocks fall 50% from their highs like they did during the Great Recession, you have to consider what those highs will be.

Some people who pull out too early miss out on all of their gains which cuts back on the potential return you would get if you are right about the recession and if you re-enter the stock market and individual companies at the right time. There are a lot of unknowns, second-thoughts, and sleepless nights if you take this approach.

This is why I have been advocating dividend investing throughout the book. If you feel stressed about investing in stocks, you need to take a breather, really think about what goes into your decision process, and re-evaluate. If you think this is stressful, your return is going to suffer even more.

Utilize a solid strategy that makes you confident regardless of the current economic outlook and you will likely do fine in the long-term.

Understand What You Buy

The most important criteria for investing in dividend stocks is to understand a stock before you buy it. This is part of the reason I have emphasized conducting research. Research can help you understand a company that you currently do not understand.

However, there is an important point about understanding a company. Understanding a company and knowing what a company does are two different things. You can know what Fiverr offers to existing customers. Fiverr is a website that allows you to buy services for as little as $5.

However, do you truly understand the business model?

Do you understand their KPIs? Do you understand the growth opportunities? Do you know what their new initiatives are? Do you know how they profit or lose money?

A more obvious example is Amazon. When most people think of Amazon, they think of retail. People who truly understand Amazon the company also think about AWS because that currently makes up more than half of Amazon's revenue.

Amazon only recently began allowing people to advertise on their platform while Facebook and Google were early to the game. Advertising is a great growth opportunity for Amazon.

Again, this is why you do the research. Just read through articles from good authors for 15-30 minutes each day and you'll know the essentials about the company you're considering. Looking at financials gives you a clear picture of past performance and the outlook, but if you read a little bit each day, you'll quickly get ahead of the game.

Conclusion

Dividend investing requires a long-term outlook. While it is possible to buy growth companies and reap massive short-term rewards, growth companies require that you time the market. Some growth companies become very successful and reap massive returns, but until those returns are realized (or if they are realized at all), it is a more risky venture.

All investments have different risk and reward ratios. Some investments are high risk and high reward. This is where you'll find many growth stocks with Bitcoin belonging in its own category of high risk and high reward.

Dividend stocks fall lower on the list of high risk and high reward. The risk is less which means the reward is also less. Your typical dividend stock isn't likely to double in value this year, but wait 20 years and the dividend income will look far more amazing than it does now.

U.S. Treasuries are among the lowest risk but also among the lowest rewards. One of the few investment vehicles that is less risky than U.S. Treasuries is leaving your money in the bank and getting the annual interest…but that interest doesn't stand a chance against inflation. You'd also need a microscope to see the interest rate the bank gives you on your saved money.

Some investing vehicles present low risks and high rewards. These are usually the assets that haven't changed in intrinsic value but have had their prices hit hard due to recent news. Other investments are high risk and low return. Stay away from those types of investments.

If you want to sleep easier at night and know you are gradually building up your wealth, you need assets that give you income. Dividend stocks are one of the easiest ways for anyone to get started on building their wealth. Real estate multifamily properties and rentals are also great choices if you know what you are doing. But dividend investing is a lower commitment and easier to get into. The return on dividend investing, just like the real estate, tends to be very good if you stay in it for a long period of time and invest in reliable companies.

The math behind using dividend investing to retire is sound. The only challenge is making enough money to buy enough dividend stocks so you can retire.

So if you want to speed up your retirement, you have to focus on boosting your earned income. Your job has a cap, but there is no cap to how much money a business can make. You can always create another product, look for new clients, and get more publicity. It's easier to retire on $100,000/yr than on $50,000/yr assuming expenses are the same.

Dividend investing starts with the first investment. Once you start investing in dividend stocks, it will get easier and you'll become more committed over time. In the long-term, your returns will look great if you continue to stay sharp with the news and make the right investments.

About The Author

Marc Guberti is a USA Today and WSJ bestselling author with over 100,000 students in over 180 countries enrolled in his online courses. He is the host of the Breakthrough Success Podcast and Radio Show where listeners learn how to achieve their breakthroughs. He coaches authors, speakers, and business owners on how they can attract more traffic to their content and boost revenue.

Marc also hosts the Profitable Public Speaking Podcast and Ditch The Job Podcast. All of his podcasts also have separate YouTube channels.

If you enjoyed this book, make sure you subscribe to my YouTube channel (just search "Marc Guberti" on YouTube) for videos that will help you gain more visibility and revenue with the content you're creating.

It would be greatly appreciated if you could leave a quick review for this book on Amazon if you found it to be helpful.

Marc's Other Books

Are you looking for your next book? If so, Marc has written over 20 books which can all be found on Amazon. Here's some of what is waiting for you if you search "Marc Guberti" on Amazon…

Content Marketing Secrets — Discover the key secrets for getting massive traffic and revenue

"This book is a getting-it-done guide for going big in small, manageable steps. Marc has put the playbook together for you." --**Andy Crestodina, author of Content Chemistry**

Podcast Domination — Discover the ultimate podcasting strategies that will help you launch, grow, and monetize your show

"Thorough coverage of the subject. Many books in the topic seem to be teasers to sell premium content. This book is not like that - he covers all topics." — **Amazon Review**

The Wealthy Author — Discover how to use books to grow your brand and earn passive income.

"If you want to learn more about making more with your books, this is the book you need!" — **Michelle Kulp, best-selling author**

<u>YouTube Decoded</u> — Discover how to create engaging You-Tube videos that attract visibility and revenue to your business.

"YouTube is a mystery to many and thanks to Marc's tenacity and in-depth focus on education, YouTube Decoded is the book that really helped our team to understand the power of the platform. Well written, worth picking up." — **Mark Asquith, founder of Rebel Base Media**

<u>Build Your Authority Platform</u> — Discover how to leverage digital marketing strategies to build your tribe of followers.

"In this straight-forward book, I got some real clarity and actionable advice to take all the content I've been building over the past few years and make it work for me. I also have direction and a plan for what I build going forward." — **Bryan Falchuk, bestselling author of Do A Day**

Want To Get Featured In A Future Book?

Would you like to put your story and brand in front of 1000s of people? If so, you may consider getting featured in one of my future books.

I write new books each month and offer feature slots for people who want their story told in a future book.

Right now, you can use the coupon code DIVIDEND to save $50 if you buy a featured slot for a future book.

Get your feature here —> marcguberti.com/bookfeature

I primarily write books around investing and business growth strategies. If you have any questions about whether your story is a good fit for a future book, please email me marc@marcguberti.com and we will see if we can make it work.

www.ingramcontent.com/pod-product-compliance
Lightning Source LLC
Chambersburg PA
CBHW020553220526
45463CB00006B/2292